"Always be Yourself

Unless you can be a Frog

Then always be a Frog"

Julie
Esther

Frogs

Weird and Wonderful

Written and Illustrated
By Leah Ingledew

Did you know that there are lots of **weird** and **wonderful** frogs in the world?

Frogs have been around for millions of years and there are thousands of different kinds!

Let me tell you a little bit more about us...

Some of us are big...

This **Goliath Frog** is the biggest frog in the world and it lives in Western Africa, near fast-flowing rivers and waterfalls.

It's around 30cm long and weighs up to 3.3kg.

That's about the same size as a cat!

Some of us are small.

This tiny frog in Madagascar is one of the smallest in the world.

It's probably the same size as your fingernail!

We eat mostly insects. We use our long tongues to catch them, but our tongues are not as long as you might think. They are about one third of the length of our bodies.

We can shoot out our tongues and catch an insect faster than you can blink!

How long is your tongue?

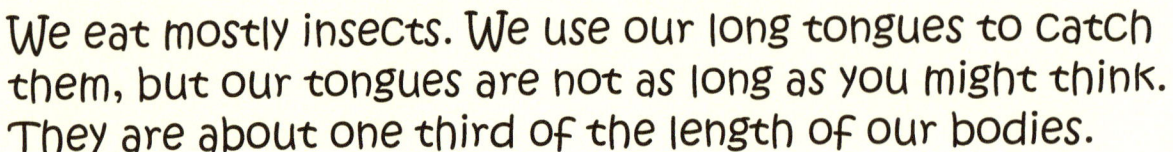

The Goliath Frog eats insects, small animals, snakes, other frogs, mice, fish, crabs, snails, worms and more.

It can jump three metres to catch food!

Frogs are amphibians.
Amphibian means 'two-lives'.
One in the water and one on land.

As froglets, they can now leave the water and live on the land.

Tadpoles breathe through gills, like fish, until their lungs develop.

They eat algae and water fleas.

What's the difference between a frog...

- Skin is smooth and looks wet. It needs to stay in damp places because it loses water easily.

- Back legs are longer than their head and body.

- Frog spawn is laid in jelly-like clumps.

- Tadpoles are thin with gold spots.

Common Frog

...and a toad?

- Skin is dry and bumpy. Toads can go to drier places because their skin is more waterproof.

- Back legs are shorter than their head and body.

- Toad spawn is laid in long strings.

- Tadpoles are fatter and black with a fatter tail.

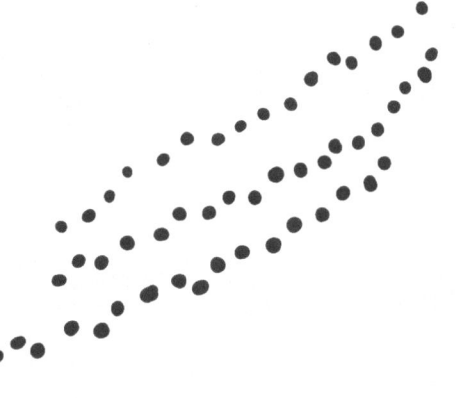

Common Toad

Most of us are nocturnal and are more active at night. We can still see in colour in the dark!

The **Red Eyed Tree Frog** has sticky pads on the ends of their fingers and toes. These help the frog hold on to things.

They keep their eyes closed to hide from things that might want to eat them.

But if they are seen, they open their eyes and jump away, showing their colourful sides and dazzling predators, until they can hide again.

Poison dart frogs are brightly coloured and some have patterns. One Golden Poison Dart Frog has enough poison to kill 10 people!

A long time ago, hunters in Columbia used the poison from this frog for hunting birds, monkeys and other small animals.

Strawberry Poison Dart Frogs are often red, but come in other colours too. This one looks like it's wearing jeans!

Frogs don't make the poison themselves, they get it from the ants and other insects they eat, and store it in glands underneath their skin.

Even baby frogs are poisonous!

The Golden Poison Dart Frog is one of the most poisonous animals alive.

We live near water, but not in the sea, because it's too salty.

We are cold-blooded, so we become the same temperature as the environment around us.

Three claws on their back feet help to tear food apart.

The African Clawed Frog lives in lakes, rivers, ponds and swamps in Africa.

They are speedy swimmers and can swim in all directions.

They have no tongue, no teeth, no eyelids and no eardrums!

We live under the ground, above the ground, in the water and even in the trees!

Most of us hibernate (a long Winter sleep) if it gets cold and we can also estivate (short Summer sleep) if it gets too hot or dry.

The Glass Frog lives in the trees in South America.

Most of them are only a few centimetres long.

- Heart
- Gall bladder
- Intestines
- Vein

They have thin skin and you can see their organs through the skin on their bellies.

Sometimes you can even see the heart beating!

We live all over the world, on every continent except Antarctica. It's too cold there for us.

This **Wallace's Flying Frog** lives in tropical jungles and glides from tree to tree.

The **Wallace's Flying Frog** spreads out their webbed feet to glide through the air after they jump.

They also have flaps of skin on the sides of their bodies to help them glide.

They can glide for 15 metres!

We need rainforests and jungles, rivers and streams.

We don't want to end up extinct like the dinosaurs!

What is your favourite frog?

Scan and print this frog pattern or use a square piece of paper. Try making lots of frogs and create an army of frogs!

You can also scan and print the next page of insects and other things frogs eat. Feed your frogs by flicking them onto the page and see how many your frog will land on.

Follow these folding instructions to make your own frog!

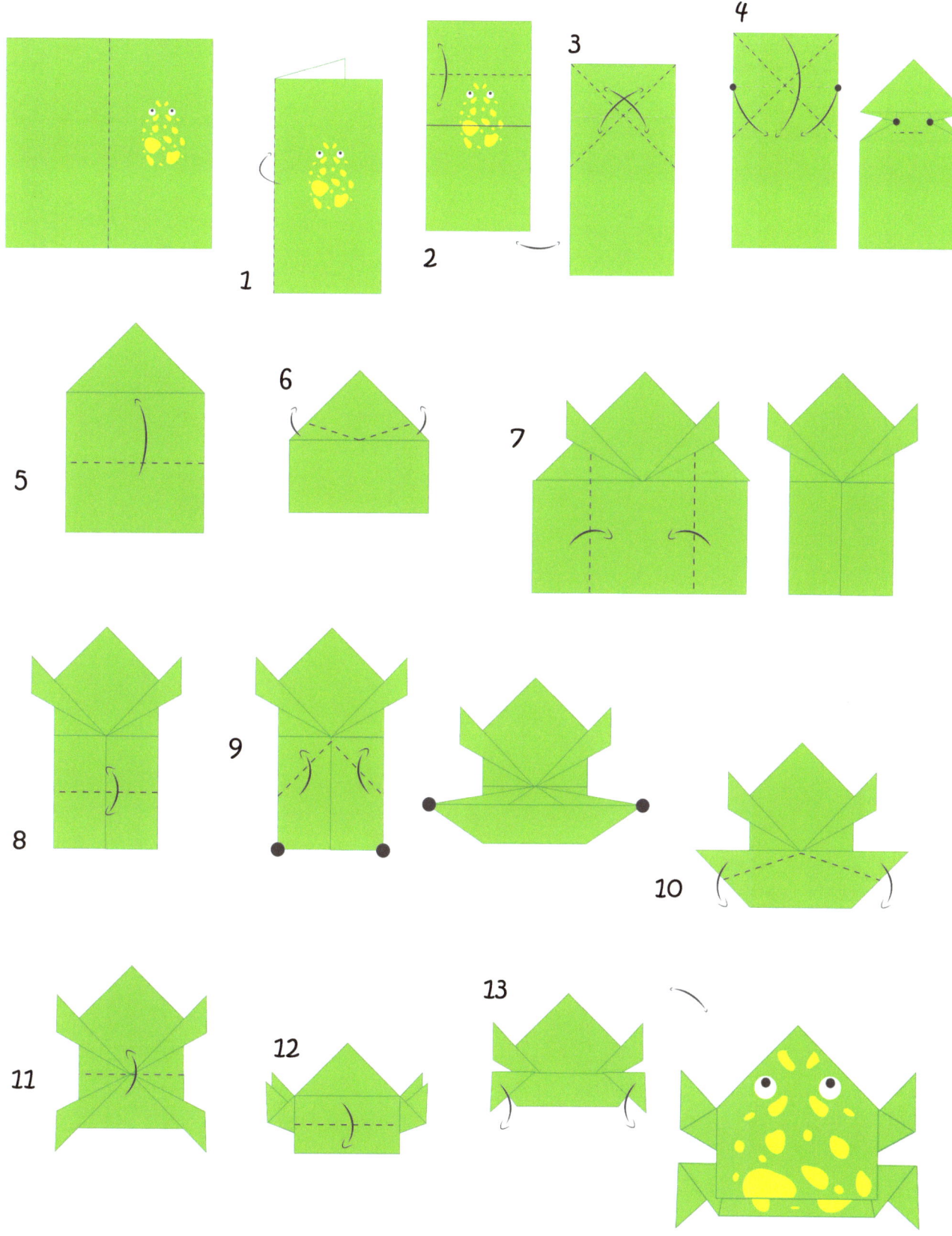

CPSIA information can be obtained
at www.ICGtesting.com
Printed in the USA
LVHW071920271020
669969LV00003B/14